I.S.A.M. Monographs: Number 9

Two Men
for
Modern Music

E. Robert Schmitz and Herman Langinger

VIVIAN PERLIS

I.S.A.M. Monographs: Number 9

Two Men
for
Modern Music

E. Robert Schmitz and Herman Langinger

VIVIAN PERLIS

Institute for Studies in American Music
Department of Music
School of Performing Arts
Brooklyn College
of The City University of New York

Copyright © 1978 by Vivian Perlis
ISBN 0-914678-09-4
Printed in the United States of America

Published by Institute for Studies in American Music
Department of Music, School of Performing Arts,
Brooklyn College of the City University of New York
Brooklyn, New York 11210

173492

PREFACE

The annual Senior Research Fellowship of the Institute for Studies in American Music was held during 1976-77 by Vivian Perlis. In addition to pursuing her ongoing research projects under the Fellowship and directing a seminar on "The Great Innovators in American Music," Ms. Perlis delivered a pair of public lectures titled as is the present monograph. (The lectures were read at Brooklyn College on 3 May and 10 May 1977.) Ms. Perlis has revised the lectures for publication and has added the illustrations, almost all of which are herewith published for the first time.

Vivian Perlis has been active as a teacher, harpist, librarian, and writer on American music. At Yale University, she is assistant curator of the Charles Ives Collection, senior research associate in the School of Music, and lecturer in American Studies. She is perhaps best known as a pioneer, among musicologists, in utilizing the techniques of oral history and as the founding director of the Oral History, American Music project at Yale. Among the significant results of this project have been her prize-winning book, *Charles Ives Remembered: An Oral History* (Yale University Press, 1974) and the bonus disc of interview excerpts in the Columbia Records album (which she co-produced) *Charles Ives: The 100th Anniversary* (M4-32504; 1974). She also was co-producer of the CRI disc *Music of Leo Ornstein* (SD 339; 1975).

H. Wiley Hitchcock, Director
Institute for Studies in American Music
21 September 1978

CONTENTS

Preface   v

Introduction   1

Before World War I   3

1918 - 1928   6

1929 - 1940   22

Notes   32

ILLUSTRATIONS

Robert Schmitz, 1913   4

Herman Langinger, 1927   8

Sergei Prokofiev and Lina Llubera, 1926   13

Letter from Alban Berg to Robert Schmitz   14-15

Maurice Ravel and John Barrymore, 1928   17

Page in Bartók's hand from draft of folk music article   19

Monique Leduc, Pierre Monteux, Schmitz, Jean Leduc,
  Darius Milhaud, Germaine Schmitz   21

Autograph manuscript page of a march by Henry Cowell   25

Autograph manuscript of "Soliloquy" by Charles Ives   26

"Soliloquy" from *Thirty-Four Songs*   27

Letter from Carl Ruggles to Herman Langinger   28-29

Introduction

A look at modern music between the two world wars reveals a complex picture of composers, performers, societies, and promoters bound together by a devotion to new music
and a determination to aid in its dissemination. Two men in this picture were Elie Robert
Schmitz and Herman Langinger. Schmitz, a French concert pianist and conductor, was
recognized both here and abroad as performer, teacher, and entrepreneur. As founder-
director of the Pro-Musica Society, Schmitz established over forty chapters, all dedicated
to the performance of little-known music. Langinger, after emigrating as a boy to America
from his native Austria, struggled to make a living in music. He learned the craft of music
engraving and eventually became the engraver for the publications of Henry Cowell's New
Music Society. Schmitz was the older of the two men; he was born in 1889 (and died in
1949). Langinger was born in 1908 and is still active as a music printer and owner of the
Highland Music Press in Hollywood, California.

These two men did not know each other. In fact, they had little in common except for
an overwhelming enthusiasm for new music that led both of them to dedicate the greater
part of their lives to its promotion. Why choose to speak about these two unrelated figures from the many involved in modern music during the first half of the century?

When the historian G. M. Trevelyan defined the dynamic nature of history, he declared
that each age writes history anew.[1] While the facts of the past do not change, our discov-
ery and our comprehension of them do change constantly. This is particularly true when
hidden information and artifacts are found and brought to light. The addition of "new"
material to existing documentation results in a change of relationships, a shift in emphasis,
and a thickening of texture. Langinger is mentioned briefly in only two recent publications,[2] and Schmitz is remembered primarily as director of Pro-Musica, although he was
well recognized as a pianist and teacher during his lifetime.[3] However, important collec-

tions relating to each of these men have recently been discovered in the course of interviews conducted for an oral history project on Charles Ives.[4] These newly found treasures add considerably to the existing information on Schmitz and Langinger, and on the Pro-Musica and New Music societies.[5] This is why I have chosen these two men as the subjects of this essay, using the interviews and collections as sources. From the intricate tapestry of people and events in modern music, these two lines will be lifted and examined, and as a result they will gain in intensity and color. When they are set back into the over-all picture, it will have an added dimension. Schmitz and Langinger, as part of the same fabric, will not be viewed as isolated and separate strands, but as contrapuntal lines, independent but simultaneous, in a multilayered, polyrhythmic world.

It is not an entirely novel idea to think of history as contrapuntal events. In his *Music in the Renaissance,* Gustave Reese writes, "If there were such a thing as polyphony in prose, it would obviously be a godsend to the writer of history"—but, Reese reminds us, language is far less adaptable to contrapuntal treatment than music.[6] Nevertheless, we have become so familiar with multiplicity and the coexistence of disparate elements, among other innovations in the arts, that we no longer find them shocking or disruptive. Consider, for example, the pluralism of Jackson Pollock, the inclusivity of Willem DeKooning, and the multilayering of Charles Ives. Polyharmony, polyrhythm, collage, abstraction—these and other innovative ideas are now understood without difficulty when applied to art works. Moreover, we have been witness to artists' revolt against the division of art from life, and against the separation of one art from another, In the past, we had been trained to separate our senses; now, we are taught to perceive music as "spatial" and painting as "contrapuntal." Perhaps we have reached a time when we can think of history, too, in such terms. Since Dilthey's criticism of the scientific approach to history, historians have been moving away from fragmentation.[7] The movement toward cultural history has followed the artists' lead in blurring definitions between genres and in questioning (as have Marcel Duchamp and John Cage) the distinction between art and life. Cultural history so intensified its demands for incorporating the amalgam of life into the historical narrative that by 1959 Hans Meyerhoff could declare, "The subject matter of history is human life in its totality and multiplicity. It is the historian's aim to portray the bewildering, unsystematic variety of historical forms—people, nations, cultures, customs, institutions, songs, myths, and thoughts—in their unique, living expressions and in the process of continuous growth and transformation. This aim is not unlike the artist's."[8]

Before World War I

E. Robert Schmitz was a talented protégé of Debussy. He had won two prizes at the Paris Conservatory and had caught the attention of Paris, which was wide open to the arts during the pre-World War I years. The music world welcomed this attractive young upstart with his enthusiasm for new music and new ideas.

Schmitz had toured the United States as early as 1910-11, as accompanist to the opera singers Emma Eames, Maggie Teyte, and Leo Slezak, travelling by train, greatly impressed with what the Europeans called "the American legend." From 1911 to 1914 Schmitz and his youthful bride, Germaine, directed the Association Musicale Moderne et Artistique, a group of young and talented musicians, some recently graduated from the Paris Conservatory; they organized an orchestra, a chorus, an a cappella octet, a woodwind ensemble, and a string quartet. Germaine also organized a *comité actif*—a working board—composed of the critics Louis Vuillemin, Emile Vuillermoz, and Michael Calvocoressi, the trumpet virtuoso Ben Vanesek, and the Greek composer Emile Riadis. Schmitz, as director and conductor, had the interest of established composers like Camille Saint-Saëns and Vincent D'Indy, and financial assistance from Germaine's family.

In 1914 the Association Musicale Moderne et Artistique took the name of the Association des Concerts Schmitz, and its scope was broadened: the chorus reached one hundred and fifty members and the orchestra ninety-four, of whom forty were prize-winners from the Conservatory. Their concerts emphasized little-known music, and there were many premiere performances, among them Claude Debussy's *Première rapsodie* for clarinet and orchestra, Albert Roussel's *Evocations,* Paul Le Flem's *Crepuscules d'Amour,* and Darius Milhaud's *Suite Symphonique.* Years later, Milhaud recalled the occasion of the first orchestral presentation ever given of his works: "He [Schmitz] provided me with the opportunity of hearing my music when he conducted this symphonic suite. I had no unpleasant surprise, but was reassured at the very first rehearsal; my orchestra sounded exactly as I had wanted it to sound." [9]

In addition to concerts, Schmitz initiated a unique series of recital-lectures, called "The Musical Geography," which were designed to further internationalism in music. Each lecture traced the music of a country from its folk origin to the works of its contemporary composers, the music being illustrated by a small group of chamber musicians. Leo Ornstein assisted in a lecture on Greece, playing works by Riadis, and Calvocoressi led one of the most memorable programs on Austria, emphasizing the importance of Arnold Schoenberg's twelve-tone method at a time when critics were almost unanimously hostile

Robert Schmitz as conductor in 1913. (Schmitz Collection)

to Schoenberg's ideas.

During these pre-war years, Schmitz made frequent appearances as concert pianist through-out Europe. He had memorized all of Debussy's piano works and performed them often. In the fall of 1912 he left Paris for a three-month tour in Holland and Belgium, returning home to conduct the final concert of his orchestra at the Salle Gaveau. He also gave a great deal of time to the demands of his teacher, as accompanist and coach for Debussy's interpreters. (The real-life Pelléas and Mélisande, David Devries and Maggie Teyte, worked directly with Debussy and Schmitz.) [10]

Schmitz's music activities, diverse and adventurous, ceased totally and abruptly in 1914. The members of the Association des Concerts Schmitz became members of the infantry and air force. Schmitz himself spent three years at the front. Once a shrapnel burst sev-ered the ligaments in his left hand, and in 1917 he was hospitalized for eight months due to severe gassing and fatigue. Not until after the armistice of 1918 was he to resume his musical career in the United States, where his experiences and contacts from the early years in Paris proved to be invaluable.

As for Herman Langinger in the years preceding World War 1: he lived for the first ten years of his life in Spas, Austria, where he was born. His grandfather was the mayor and the rabbi of the town, and his father was studying to be a rabbi. He was also a natural musician and composer. As a young boy, Langinger learned to play the violin, without any idea that someday he would become involved with the most avant-garde music of this century. He described this early experience in an interview:

> I did not study music with my father. He was here in the States
> during the war—he came before us. When we were growing up, my brother
> and I were taken by my father to an old man from Vienna, a professor of
> music who had retired to Spas. My father bought us little violins. The pro-
> fessor gave us lessons and we started to practice. From then on, we could
> never stop. So much so that my older sister wanted to learn too and I showed
> her by rote.
>
> In those days, among the older Jewish people, if anyone was showing
> an interest in becoming a musician, he was an outcast, a bum. We were all
> living together in my grandfather's big house, and when my grandmother
> heard some noise, she opened the door and asked, "What is that?" My mother
> was so glad we were practicing: "They are going to become violin players."

"Not in my family," grandmother shouted. Music was only for the temple, and, oh my gosh, not for a respectable person and not on a violin! We had to sneak out for lessons and have our sister watch to see where Grandma was.

We had to run away from the Cossacks, leaving our violins and everything. When we came back to Spas, the Armistice came, but the Revolution started between Polish people and the Russians. We received our passports, and we dashed away. [11]

1918-1928

There are days of such moment in history that they are recalled in vivid detail years later by those who went through them. Everyone alive at the time remembers where they were and what they were doing on Pearl Harbor Day or on the day John F. Kennedy was shot. Such a day was Armistice Day, 11 November 1918. Where were the major figures of modern music on Armistice Day?

Schoenberg and Ives were both forty-four years old in 1918. They had been composing for many years. When the Armistice was declared, Schoenberg was teaching and composing in Vienna. Ives had virtually stopped composing; on Armistice Day he was recuperating in New York from a serious heart attack of six weeks earlier. Stravinsky, already famous, was in Switzerland preparing to return to Paris. Leo Ornstein, age twenty-six and hailed as the greatest "futurist" composer, was shocking audiences and critics in New York with his wildly avant-garde pieces. [12] Varèse was conducting the New Symphony Orchestra in New York, while Carl Ruggles was directing an orchestra in Winona, Minnesota. Charles Seeger, a conscientious objector during World War I, was at his father's house in Patterson, New York, building the first known automobile trailer in the country. [13] Seeger's former student in California, Henry Cowell, was a twenty-one-year-old conductor of an army band at Camp Crane in Allentown, Pennsylvania.

Elie Robert Schmitz was twenty-nine in 1918. From an interview with his daughter, Monique Schmitz Leduc, we know exactly where he was on Armistice Day:

Father had an honorable discharge, and since Grandfather was going to the States on business, Father made reservations to go at the same time, to give his services to the American Committee of the French Restoration. But when they got to Le Havre the sailors just wouldn't sail—something was

going on, and there were rumors that Germany was collapsing. They just had
to wait in port, and they were there when Armistice was declared. This was
followed by an eighteen-day trip crisscrossing the Atlantic with Spanish flu
aboard and corpses being thrown overboard right and left.

Father was able to practice some, and although during the war years he
was out of it, he had discussed matters of energy and trajectory with mathe-
maticians and engineers, which made Father come to the idea that the way
one learned piano was terribly haphazard. All this instinct and inspiration
bit! Father's book [14] evolved from the bull sessions he had with men at the
front, discussing scientific questions aimed toward the elimination of waste
motion. . . .

When the family finally arrived in the States, Grandfather's business
contract was not honored, and it must have been a very bad time for the
whole family. Father had some contacts, and he began performing a great
deal with other musicians in New York and across the country. This was the
real beginning of Father's American career. [15]

Tracing the lines of our two men following the Armistice, we find Langinger as a teenager
resettled in Chicago, struggling with a foreign language, studying music, and earning a
living as an apprentice at the firm of Rayner, Dalheim, music engravers. His pay was only
eight dollars a week, but according to Langinger it was "like being in school, and they
paid me on top of it. Everything fell into my lap—it was hard work, but I loved it." [16]
Langinger taught violin and harmony after hours. He organized the Langinger String
Quartet, and by 1923 his small group of musicians grew into an orchestra of thirty members. *The Metronome* music magazine ran a picture and a short article describing his
accomplishments. [17]

In 1927 Langinger left Chicago for New York to study violin with Leopold Lichtenberg
and to work for Joseph Ranc, a prestigious music engraver in the Carl Fischer building.

When I came to New York, those boys were really laughing at me. No-
body knew music. I was the only student. And here comes Leopold Auer,
Leopold Godowsky. I didn't behave like a big shot. I never do. But they
were making fun of me because here comes a yokel from Chicago, and he
knows it all. "Here big shot, if you know how to do it, go ahead." Well, any-
thing that was difficult, I undertook. And I wasn't angry about it—I welcomed that.

Herman Langinger in 1927 as conductor of the Langinger Symphony Orchestra organized by him in 1924 in Chicago. (Langinger Collection)

Then in comes Charles Ives.[18] . . . I had never seen music that revolutionary. The boss would stand over us and watch us work together and then walk away. Charles Ives's work was a mathematical problem, and this was a terrific challenge to me. Ives had sent the score [of the Fourth Symphony, second movement] to Cowell in San Francisco, but his engravers [Pacific Music Press] couldn't make heads or tails of it, so Cowell sent it to Chicago and then to Philadelphia. Same story. Then Ives took the score to Schirmer's who also couldn't make it out. Finally it went to Fischer's and Ranc gave it to me. It took me all summer [1928] to do that job. I loved it! You look at the first page and you see that this is a mathematical problem. And in the middle, you've got quarter-tone piano. I had to design a special square note for that. After this piece, I did other music for Ives. He was happy to find someone who spoke the language. I remember that he said, "It's a godsend to me." I worked directly from his writings with no copyist's scores.[19]

As for E. Robert Schmitz in the years following 1918: it did not take him long to resume his concert career after arriving in New York. The *New York Times* wrote on his arrival that Schmitz had "come to make zee propaganda for French music." From the programs of his concerts in the first few years, he clearly did much more than that. In the winter of 1919 he played John Alden Carpenter's *Concertino* with the Boston Symphony Orchestra. (In June of 1920 he introduced Parisian audiences to it.) [20] In other concerts he presented works by Schoenberg, Ravel, Prokofiev, Milhaud, and Honegger. Richard L. Stokes wrote in the *New York World* following the New York premiere of Manuel de Falla's *Nights in the Garden of Spain,* with Schmitz as soloist with the Philharmonic, "An electrical touch is the gift of E. Robert Schmitz, French pianist. The music that tingles from his hands is like the crackling Gallic prose in which Dumas celebrates the exploits of D'Artagnan." [21]

Schmitz's enthusiasm for new ideas extended in other directions than performance. In his teaching and performing he continued to apply scientific principles and to experiment with instruments that would enlarge expressive possibilities for the performer. He talked to Thomas Edison in 1920 at the inventor's home in New Jersey. As a result of that conversation, Schmitz and Edison worked together in the Edison studios for "a week's experimenting."[22] An article printed in the *Commercial Tribune,* Cincinnati, and the *Detroit Free Press,* 20 June 1920, reported some of their conversation:

THOMAS EDISON DISCUSSES SOME INTERESTING
PHASES OF PIANISM OF THE FUTURE

Mr. Edison—That piece of Debussy's was very fine . . . but, you know I am half-and-half with regard to Debussy.

Mr. Schmitz—Perhaps that is for the same reason that Debussy himself was half-and-half when he heard his own piano music. Debussy and I were good friends, and he told me often that he was grievously dissatisfied with the way the piano was rendering his writings. He really wrote for an instrument in advance of the piano.

Mr. Edison (interested)—His compositions anticipated a new instrument?

Mr. Schmitz—Not an unprecedented thing with creative musicians. . . Debussy demands a quality that is impossible to secure on the present pianoforte.

Mr. Edison (interrupting)—Do you know the quality I want the piano to have? An end to hammering. Sound a note or a chord without the initial bang. A piano note that will attack smoothly, as a violin note does, or a flute note. That may be swelled. And yet of the true vibrating piano-string quality. I have thought of this often.

Mr. Schmitz—You have it. Debussy's harmonies demand precisely that sort of treatment. . . . Debussy wrote really for a revolutionized piano. . . Debussy in his music fully anticipated the new invention. . . .

Mr. Edison (meditatively)—I think it will come. Did Debussy ever talk to you about a revolutionized pianoforte?

Mr. Schmitz—He often spoke of the need of a piano that would be free from the hammering attack, but he never thought of the mechanical side of the problem.

Mr. Edison (grimly)—A somewhat important side. . . .

Mr. Schmitz—During the war, while I was at the front, I often discussed with prominent engineers the possibility of revolutionizing the piano through electricity. . . .

Mr. Edison (smiling)—The advanced composers have set the pace esthetically. The inventive mind will have to follow with a little practical work.

Mr. Schmitz—You say that you have thought about a revolutionized piano?

Mr. Edison—Yes, and I shall think about it further.

The greatest of inventors lapsed into thoughtful silence. E. Robert Schmitz wrinkled his triangular face . . . and wondered whether the problem that Debussy set forth in fact might not be on the way to realization in the brain of Edison.

After touring the United States in 1920 to survey the music known and played in each area, Germaine and Robert Schmitz were determined to find a way of bringing composers to America for nationwide tours, and of introducing European audiences to American music. They sought support from Schmitz's earlier admirers and succeeded in launching an international society in 1920. At first, when exchanges were primarily between France and America, the society was called the Franco-American Musical Society. Later, in 1923, after its scope broadened, the name was changed to Pro-Musica, Incorporated. This association was to become one of the most powerful of several societies actively engaged in promoting new music. By 1930, Pro-Musica had over forty thriving chapters, in such cities as New York, Boston, Cincinnati, Cleveland, Chicago, Minneapolis, St. Paul, Salt Lake City, Seattle, Kansas City, Denver, Berkeley, San Francisco, Los Angeles, Montreal, London, Paris, Berlin, Tokyo, Shanghai, Honolulu, and Moscow. Schmitz performed in all of these places, winning patrons and audiences over to support of Pro-Musica chapters. His daughter put it this way:

> Father felt, in doing all his tours, that it would be remarkable if one could establish something which would not be centered in New York, already a privileged city. Chapters throughout the United States and maybe Canada could really back tours of composers. You could make it possible for people in Oklahoma or Nebraska to know what an actual live composer was like—to see him, hear him, and discuss music with him—and then become terribly excited about his music.

> One reason for Pro-Musica's success was that Father gave a great deal of his time to it. He did a lot of foot work, and he was a convincing person. He had an agreeable personality—very generous, and rather fun—not a difficult person to know, and he had good committees working in all these different places, people who really were quite serious about it so that the responsibility was shared. Each place had only to guarantee so much to bring someone like Ravel or Bartók to their town. The reception in the most unlikely places was excellent. This was something that always astonished Father. In places that we, as European snobs, felt would never have good reactions, you could find people who suddenly fall totally in love with Poulenc! It was a very strange phenomenon in the twenties. It was a sort of crazy and wide-open American scene.[23]

In its first few seasons, the Franco-American/Pro-Musica Society presented French music performed by Schmitz, Carlos Salzedo, and Georges Barrère. Nadia Boulanger lectured on contemporary music for several Pro-Musica chapters when she was in the States in

1923, and Alexander Tansman came from Paris to do recitals. The Paris chapter heard
American music by Marion Bauer, Charles Griffes, and Louis Gruenberg. The *Franco-
American Musical Society Bulletin* (later retitled *Pro-Musica Quarterly*) was activated in
1923, with Ely Jade (the *nom de plume* of Germaine Schmitz) as editor and Greta
Torpadie as assistant editor. In that year also, the first of a series of yearly international
Referendum Concerts, which featured programs suggested by the society's International
Advisory Board, was initiated.

Schmitz made four tours a year, two in Europe and two in the United States and Canada,
driving across country. On these tours, he performed, taught students and small groups
of teachers, and kept track of the Pro-Musica chapters. In Europe Schmitz convinced
outstanding composers in each place he visited to serve on the International Board. For
example, in 1924 when he played concerts in Vienna, Schmitz searched out Alban Berg
and Egon Wellesz, invited them to join the board, and requested suggestions for future
Pro-Musica programs. (See pages 14-15 for Berg's response.) When touring the States,
Robert and Germaine searched town archives for programs of concerts performed in the
past ten to fifteen years, tabulating the results to determine the right balance of modern
and classical music for each place. Pro-Musica's programs and presentations became more
diverse and far too numerous to chronicle here but for a few highlights. Alfredo Casella
toured in 1925 with lecture-recitals on the condition of contemporary Italian music. A
major event of 1926 was Prokofiev's tour, with an opening recital in St. Paul that was
repeated before ten other chapters. Prokofiev requested that his wife, the renowned
soprano Lina Llubera, appear with him. He wrote to Schmitz, "I will definitely not give
my melodies to local artists as they will not sing them as I want them sung and I will not
be able to train a new singer in each city." In answer to Pro-Musica's desire that he give
lectures along with his recitals, he said, "How little you know me! I hate lectures and
the setting forth of theories. . . . In my opinion any composer who launches into
theories kills himself as a composer."[24] In 1926 Schmitz called on other musicians he
had known in Paris to come to the States (he had met Prokofiev in pre-war Paris and
played his First Piano Concerto with the Concerts Schmitz). Darius Milhaud made an
extensive tour, as did Henry Eichheim, a quartet from Belgium, and the Pro Arte Quartet.

1927 has been declared a turning point in the development of civilization.[25] It was a
year of national radio networks, underwater tunnels, talking films, and the establishment
of radio-telephone service between New York and London, San Francisco and Manila;
and it was the year Lindbergh crossed the Atlantic. In American music, there were also
historic events—Jerome Kern's *Showboat* opened on Broadway; Duke Ellington opened
at the Cotton Club; George Antheil's *Ballet mécanique* scandalized audiences at Carnegie
Hall; and the world premiere of the prelude and second movement of Ives's Fourth

Sergei Prokofiev with his wife, the soprano Lina Llubera, at the close of the composer's first American tour in 1926. (Schmitz Collection)

Vienna 25 of May 1924

To the Franco American Musical Society Inc.
130 West 42nd Street New York

Mr E. Robert Schmitz had the Kindness during his stay
in Vienna to ask us, we should propose some
Works as member of the advisory board, which
would be apt for the concerts of the society
After a careful choice we propose the following
Works, which we are sending by the editors or,
If Msc. by the composers.
Regarding works in Mscrpt the authors are expecting
a salary for the first performance.

The answer we are expecting in a double copy
to our addresses

Yours very truly

Egon Wellesz
Vienna XIX Kaasgrabeng. 12

Alban Berg
Vienna XIII
Trauttmansdorffg. 27

A letter from Alban Berg to Schmitz signed by Berg and Wellesz. (Schmitz Collection)

(Letter continued on p. 15.)

We are proposing the following works.

A. Berg.   Klaviersonate op 1
                  Lieder   op 2
                  Streichquatett op 3 (Salzburg 1923)
                  Clarinette s pianopiece op 5

        a Concerto for Violin s Piano an 13 wind instrum.
will be finished in autumn.

___

H Eissler   Sonata for piano

___

J.M.Hauer   Pieces for Violin s Piano   Mscpt

___

F.H.Klein   Pieces for piano „Impressions of pictures"   op 3

___

P.A.Pisk   Pieces for the piano

___

A. Webern   5 pieces for string. op 5
              6 Bagatelles   op 9
              4 Pieces Violin s Piano op 7
              3 Pieces for Cello s piano op 11
              5 Songs   op 3
              5 "   op 4
              6 Songs for Clarinette Bassclar. Violin s Cello op 14
              3 Latin songs for voice Clarinette s Bassclar. op 16
                                        Mscpt

___

E. Wellesz.   4. String quatett op 25   (Salzburg 1922)
                Sonata for Violin solo
                Sonata for Cello solo
                2 pieces for Clarinett s piano
                Suite for Solo violin, Flute Clarinet Cor anglais Bassoon
                Viola s Cello op 38   (Salzburg 1924)

Symphony, presented on the Fourth International Referendum Concert of Pro-Musica, puzzled the audience and critics at Town Hall. (Herman Langinger worked with Ives later in 1927 toward publication of the second movement for the *New Music Quarterly* issue of January 1929.) In these years before the Wall Street crash, Pro-Musica was at the height of its success, mirroring the prosperity and idealism of this period of social transformation in America. It was a time of hope, optimism, and belief in progress. A distinguished French social scientist published *America Comes of Age* in 1927.[26] It is not a coincidence that within the next year Robert Schmitz was to bring Kodály, Respighi, Bartók, and Ravel to this country for the first time.

Since 1922, Schmitz had been wooing Ravel for Pro-Musica. Early in 1928 the French composer was finally convinced to make the tour. Schmitz wrote about how this came about:

> I remember how Ravel exploded when I ventured my conviction that the new world would be enriched if he were to interpret his music for our chapters. "Ravel as a pianist?" he cried. "You would have me compete with your American circuses?" I ended up by telling him that his tour would be a tremendous blow in favor of modern music. I could tell that I was making progress.
>
> It was then that my wife scored with a practical note. She hesitantly murmured, "You would make much money." "Really now?. . ." His uplifted eyebrow was a clear sign of interest. To my wife's discomfort and my own amazement, I heard myself saying that I would guarantee him ten thousand dollars for a three-months tour. "C'est beaucoup d'argent!" Ravel could not believe that people thousands of miles away would be eager to see him—much less pay to hear his mediocre piano playing. Nevertheless, the agreement was signed and we were left with the question of how to raise the ten thousand dollars.[27]

The full amount could not of course be raised from the annual dues—five dollars a year—paid by Pro-Musica members. Upon his return to the states, Schmitz convinced the Mason & Hamlin company to give five thousand dollars in return for Ravel's playing a Mason & Hamlin piano exclusively on the tour.

Following Ravel's agreement to make the tour, extensive correspondence and complications ensued. Ravel's manager insisted on an additional twelve hundred dollars before he would relinquish rights and payment for the American tour. Ravel confirmed his reluc-

Ravel in Hollywood with John Barrymore during his American tour in 1928,
(Schmitz Collection)

tance to leave France. He also refused to sail without a supply of his own tobacco, and he insisted that this be delivered to the boat by Pro-Musica's agent.

> I am not looking forward to crossing on a boat which, I am told, rolls heavily. My passport is in order, my cabin reserved. I am still waiting for Laberge's answer as regards the tobacco. I beg you to draw his attention to this question of which he has perhaps not understood the importance. [28]

Ravel agreed to play a number of pieces here, among them the *Sonatine*. "I worked quite a bit on the *Valses Nobles*," he wrote, "but I am certain that I will never be able to play them. Between you and me, my virtuosity will be less dazzling than the beautiful image your bulletin would have us believe." [29]

Ravel's first American appearance was as a member of the audience at Carnegie Hall on 15 January 1928. Seated in a box with Mrs. Thomas Edison and the Schmitzes, he listened while Koussevitzky conducted the Boston Symphony Orchestra in works by him. Afterward, Mrs. Edison was hostess at a reception in his honor at the Cosmopolitan Club. The following week he performed at the Gallo Theater with Greta Torpadie and Carlos Salzedo. Critics affirmed Ravel's own opinion of his playing; for example, H. B. in the *New York Evening Post* of 16 January 1928 wrote, "Judged by rigid musical standards the evening was hardly one to become a cherished memory." Nevertheless, audiences were enthusiastic, and Ravel's tour—thirty appearances as solo recitalist, conductor, and guest soloist with orchestras in New York, Cleveland, and San Francisco—was a grand success.

Schmitz first wrote to Bartók in Budapest in 1924 to invite him to make a tour in the States for Pro-Musica chapters. Bartók responded that he had made arrangements with the Baldwin piano company for a tour of ten weeks' duration to begin on 15 January 1926. [30] But because of illness he could not make the trip in 1926. Schmitz then proceeded to arrange sponsorship for the composer's arrival late in 1927. Schmitz told Winthrop Tryon in Boston:

> A new man is Bartók. He will be heard, according to present arrangements, in St. Paul, Kansas City, Denver, Portland, and San Francisco. I hope he will be able to give lectures, showing the evolution of music in Hungary. . . . Most important of all, he is a modernist composer and he will be presenting works by himself and Kodály, and other Hungarians. He can bring our audiences up to date as far as his country is concerned. You see, when we want goulash, we go to the right place for it; and when we want an Italian

Additions. #

Page 5. In diesen Tonreihen, namentlich in den pentatonischen, sind die Terz, Quint und Septime sozusagen ebenbürtig, gleichgewichtig; weil die 2. Stufe und die grosse Septime fehlen, ist die Bildung der abgedroschenen Kadenz V — I (*Ex. V*) gar nicht mög lig; dagegen, bzw. an Stelle dieser bergen die Melodien die Möglichkeit folgender Kadenz: (*Ex. 2*) aufgelöst in (*Ex. 3*).

Ja sogar vertragen viele dieser Melodien die allereinfachste Harmonisierung": einen einzigen (d.h. ein und denselben) Akkord "während der ganzen Melodie. So z. B. kann man sich folgende Melodie (eine altungarische Melodie aus Transylvanien)

Ex. 4

Parlando, ♪ = 150

Gyula-i-né é-des a-nyám! En— ged-je meg azt az e-gyet: Hogy kér-jem meg

Ká-dár Ka-tát, Job-bá-gyunk-nak szép le-á-nyát.

recht gut mit der Ostinato-Begleitung des einzigen Akkordes (*notation*) vorstellen.

A page in Bartók's hand showing corrections and additions for his article on the folk music of Hungary for *Pro-Musica Quarterly*. (Schmitz Collection)

dish, we do likewise. Along with Bartók, we shall have Casella, and from the two men we ought to get a good notion of a couple of modern tendencies that are very active and at the same time quite unlike.[31]

Bartók faced an American audience for the first time as soloist with the New York Philharmonic at Carnegie Hall on 22 December 1927, with Mengelberg conducting Bartók's own First Piano Concerto. Twenty-five concerts followed, in New York and other cities; many of them were lecture-recitals about Hungarian national music. After his return to Hungary, Bartók sent an article for *Pro-Musica Quarterly* on the folk music of Hungary.[32]

Several other societies dedicated to performance of new music were thriving in the late 1920s—the League of Composers, the Pan-American Association, and New Music. The last was based in San Francisco, where Cowell was teaching in the University of California's Extension Division. In 1928 Herman Langinger left New York for San Francisco to investigate the possibilities of starting a business of his own, and he worked there for the Pacific Music Press before founding the Golden West Music Press. Through Cowell, he met Ray Green and, later, Ingolf Dahl, who were also involved with the New Music Society. As a master engraver, Langinger was a valuable asset to the organization. Moreover, his enthusiasm for experimental music and his willingness to work with difficult and unusual scores soon put him in close touch with many of the outstanding composers whose works were submitted for publication to New Music Editions. Engraving for *New Music*, a quarterly publication, was only a small part of the business of the Golden West Music Press, but it was always the part Langinger loved best. It was a challenge that required study (a habit he maintained all his life), so he continued his private music lessons and even attended some of Cowell's classes at the University to understand more fully the experimental music chosen for publication in *New Music*.

The few years preceding the Wall Street crash gave little indication of impending disaster in the world of the arts—the crash was a sudden shock. As the Armistice of 1918 was an unforgettable event for all who experienced it, so was the crash of October 1929, and the long Depression which followed had severe effects on those supporting modern music.

Key figures in Pro-Musica: Monique Leduc, Pierre Monteux, Schmitz, Jean Leduc, Darius Milhaud, Germaine Schmitz. (Schmitz Collection)

1929-1940

In writing about the Alger Hiss case, Alistair Cooke has an excellent chapter about the 1930s. In it he points out that "We are about to look at the trials of a man who was judged in one decade for what he was said to have done in another."[33] Cooke determines that the differences between the 1920s and '30s make them almost two different periods of history: ". . . these changes in the climate of ideas . . . vary greatly in their speed and intensity. There are long stable times, like the Victorian Age in England, and short unstable periods . . . when a way of thinking and feeling crystallizes quickly and powerfully and then just as quickly goes to pieces."[34] The 1920s and '30s were just such short unstable periods, with political and economic changes making sudden shifts in the "climate of ideas." George Orwell, describing the period, wrote, "Suddenly we got out of the twilight of the gods into a sort of Boy Scout atmosphere of bare knees and community singing."[35] The abruptness of the changes made it extremely difficult for individualists such as Schmitz and Cowell to find support for their activities in modern music.

It has already been pointed out that the success of Pro-Musica depended largely on the individual efforts of Schmitz, with his attractive personality, vitality, talents, and contacts. Pro-Musica also depended on many wealthy patrons in distant cities. As this financial assistance began to wane during the Depression, Schmitz wrote to Charles Ives, who had been a faithful supporter of Pro-Musica: "People spend thousands of dollars at football games in spite of crisis, but not for music."[36] Ives answered, "I am sorry to know that Pro-Musica is not in a normal state—but it is just going through what most everything else is—too much Hoover prosperity—minus the latter. . . . All business has been in a mess— it's just a matter, I guess, of treading water till things come back."[37] A notice dated 14 October 1930 was sent to all Pro-Musica members by the secretary of the society, Sigmund Klein, announcing, "The national organization in New York is suspending for six months to a year all activities to resume in the spring of 1931 with a Japanese trio."[38]

By November of 1931 Pro-Musica was $3,000 in debt, and Schmitz was trying to bolster struggling chapters. St. Paul was abandoned; the others barely held on. With the hope of securing outside support, Schmitz tried to coordinate activities with the Society for Foreign Relations and the League of Nations. Monique Leduc described the precarious situation:

> Many friends tried to help when the financial situation threatened to break up Pro-Musica—Milhaud, Tansman, Honegger, Desormière, and Golschmann. But some of the close collaborators had died or were too tired or too old to want to carry on, and in some cases there had been difficulty in maintaining standards. It was a very large, decentralized group. Maybe one chapter is no longer interested in modern music and is just fostering local talent.

It would have taken at least a full-time person to coordinate efforts. This Father could not continue to do because it would have been financially impossible. He would have had to give up his career completely. Father did not want Pro-Musica to continue if the quality and ideals could not continue. It was very difficult for him, but eventually he asked for its disincorporation. In the long run, though, he was always convinced that it had been worthwhile. [39]

Although Pro-Musica activities were definitely curtailed, some concerts continued. In 1932 the society sponsored an all-American program in Los Angeles with music by Cowell, Copland, Ives, Sessions, and Harris. Ernst Toch made a tour that year, and in 1933 Olin Downes lectured in Seattle, while Marcel Dupré performed contemporary French works. Monteux and Casella, long-time friends and supporters, sent offers of assistance, and Milhaud wrote, "Wherever we went we met admirers and supporters of Robert Schmitz. On our return to the United States, we found that most of the branches no longer existed, which is a great pity, for Robert Schmitz had been a real pioneer of contemporary music." [40] Programs continued up to 1938, when Schmitz called for the disincorporation of Pro-Musica. His dream for an international society for modern music had been a reality for over twelve years followed by a few years of disappointment and disillusionment. The use of the name was given to a group in Montreal which is still active as a local society, but with little knowledge of Schmitz and his original concept of Pro-Musica.

Schmitz continued his activities in music. He gave concerts and made a few recordings. In the late 1930s, he recorded the Franck Quintet, and, later, a few works by Ravel and Debussy for RCA Victor. Here again he was frustrated by economic conditions, for just as he began to record the complete piano works of Debussy, the musicians' union ban in 1945 made the project impossible. Schmitz's book on Debussy was planned as one of three; unfortunately, only the first was completed and published. [41] Schmitz himself had tried his hand at composition and wrote some short piano pieces and a concerto. He edited the Chopin etudes, using them in his own teaching. Schmitz was popular and successful as a teacher through the years in many places, notably Denver and Duluth, where he conducted summer master classes to which "pianists came from eleven states and two foreign cities . . . to study with E. Robert Schmitz, the internationally known master of the piano." [42] Schmitz's interest in contemporary music extended to his teaching. Each summer there was a sight-reading contest during which students were confronted with a difficult new work. In 1931, it was music by Otto Luening and Chávez; in 1934, it was "The Alcotts" from Ives's "Concord" Sonata. The E. Robert Schmitz School was established in San Francisco in 1945. A special feature was a "Debussy Prize," offered in competition each year; it required from its contestants the sight-reading of modern music. [43]

Just as Pro-Musica had been held together by the efforts of Schmitz, so was New Music dependent on Henry Cowell. The New Music Society was small and centered in one place, and although it was always on the brink of financial disaster, it did not depend for support on wealthy patrons in distant cities during the Depression. With small amounts of money from a few people (Ives among them), New Music continued successfully in the '30s. Herman Langinger worked closely with Cowell, engraving some of the most experimental pieces for publication. Among the most difficult of these was Varèse's *Ionisation*.

> "Henry," I said, "I don't understand this *Ionisation* of Varèse. What is it all about? —a bunch of notes and single lines and percussion. But a theme, where is something?" "Well," Henry said, "come to my class and analyze it."
>
> We did just that, and I began to see a form. I became familiar with the music. We organized an orchestra and it called for two sirens, a tenor and a baritone. I was the one to get those two sirens from a store that was near me. They sold fire equipment, and I rented them. But I got mad at Henry because he had a great big gong in this, and he gave me a little finger cymbal, and I couldn't even hear myself! There were modern dancers in the performance and it was one of the finest experiences of my life.
>
> I could hear radical music so that's why I did Ives's music in the '30s. I did not know Ruggles, but I worked on his music. I met Roy Harris and did his music, and Schoenberg also. Henry depended on me for all that.[44]

New Music lost its leadership in 1936 when Cowell was suddenly arrested and sent to prison. Gerald Strang, who had been working closely with Cowell, Langinger, and a few others, tried to keep the society going. Langinger was printing and engraving music for the composers and arrangers who wrote for CBS and NBC. In 1938 when the studios moved to Los Angeles, the publishers who were dependent on them moved at the same time. Langinger's Golden West Music Press was among them. Strang had also moved to Los Angeles in order to study with Schoenberg. He and Langinger were left to manage New Music as best they could. Both were loyal to Cowell and admiring of him; they visited him regularly, but it was not possible to discuss much of the business of New Music with him. Said Langinger:

> Henry left it all in our hands. Once he wrote about a very fine flute player who was about to be released from prison. "A player from the Los Angeles Philharmonic who is here on forgery. Can you find him a job?" Now mind you, he was forging checks. I got together with Strang and we both

First page of a wedding march written by Henry Cowell in 1938 for Mr. and Mrs. Herman Langinger. Unpublished engraving by Langinger. (Langinger Collection) Permission Sidney Cowell.

Autograph manuscript page of "Soliloquy" sent by Charles Ives to Herman Langinger to engrave for *New Music Quarterly*. (Schmitz Collection) © 1933 Merion Music Inc. Used by Permission.

24
Soliloquy
or a Study in 7ths and Other Things

Adagio

When a man is sit-ting, be-fore the fire on the hearth, he says "Na-ture is a sim-ple af - fair" Then
(Chanted or half spoken and somewhat drawling, rather slowly and quietly)

Allegro

he looks out the win - dow and sees

hail storm, and he be - gins to think that

"Na - ture can't be so eas - i - ly dis - posed of!"

* If there may be two players, all the chord in each 7/8 measure may be struck; and other chords need not be rolled.

[1907]

"Soliloquy," engraved by Langinger for Ives's *Thirty-Four Songs,* Vol. 7, no. 1 (October 1933), of *New Music.* © 1933 Merion Music Inc. Used by Permission.

A letter from Carl Ruggles to Langinger about the engraving of *Evocations* for *New Music*, Vol. 18, no. 2 (January 1945). (Langinger Collection) Permission Micah Ruggles. (Letter continued on p. 29.)

April   1943

has written you about the subject matter
the title page? If not this
~~it~~ might be something like this!

36 CARL RUGGLES

30 Evocations
30
12   Chants for Piano
         3

30   Angels
12   for muted Brass.
12   4 Trumpets, and
12   3 Trombones
   April   1943

Thanking you again and
wishing you good luck,
I'm sincerely yours,
            Carl Ruggles

said, "Let's offer him a job." I don't believe in punishing people. You have to show your faith. So, when the man was released, the first thing we introduced him to was our checkbook. New Music was rich at that time—we had $150 jn the bank. We went to the bank with this man to make him treasurer. Things went fine for a few weeks, then suddenly, poof! He didn't show up. The police came to check what he did here and they brought back things they found in his possession—he had gone to Berkeley and forged checks there, but he never touched one cent of New Music's! So help me—he just forged somebody else's checks.[45]

In Los Angeles, Langinger continued his pattern of study by attending some of Schoenberg's classes with Strang. During the late '30s, Langinger became friendly with the Viennese maestro. In fact, together they made a futile attempt to bring Schoenberg's son, Georg, from Vienna on a working visa as a copyist for the Golden West Press.

When Cowell was finally released from prison on parole, he left for New York rather than remaining in California. New Music's activities gradually shifted from Los Angeles to New York. While Langinger continued to engrave music for the Quarterly, the printing was done in New York. New Music again had Cowell's care and attention. It survived until 1959, and continued to serve an important function during a time when there was little support for some of the most innovative composers. With the weakening and demise of most of the music societies, composers lost the sense of community that these groups had provided. Therefore, New Music was particularly important to composers like Ives, Ruggles, and Varèse who retreated further away from the mainstream of American musical life rather than bend with the conservative attitudes that were part of the way of life in the '30s. The radical fringe in the arts, whether Cowell's New Music or the *Partisan Review*, were decidedly not the arbiters of taste. The Great Depression had destroyed the idea of progress and brought an air of uncertainty and restlessness that was followed by a heightened sense of community as the country faced the advent of Nazism and the threat of war. Serious pursuit of the arts was marginal to the main concerns of the country. The dominant culture was a popular one—our national heroes were Mickey Mouse, Babe Ruth, Benny Goodman, and the big bands. The hopeful proclamations of 1927 for the future had turned into concentration on the present, and Siegfried's *America Comes of Age* was replaced in popularity by Dale Carnegie's *How to Win Friends and Influence People.*[46] The leading figures in the movement for modern music were forced to admit that their kind of music would have little impact on the American people or toward international cooperation.

It remains for historians to tell the tale of modern music in the first half of this century in a way that will make the reader feel that the past was once as real as the present. For this, the historian's job is threefold: first, to find artifacts and documentation (written and oral); next, to organize and interpret these materials; finally, to write the historical narrative from them. In American music, the field has been left fallow and undeveloped until recently. The remains of the past are only now being searched out, and such treasures as the Schmitz and Langinger collections have come to light. These are vital sources that put flesh on the skeletal facts of history and contribute toward a clearer understanding of the roles of the two men and their relationships to the over-all picture of music in the twentieth century.

173492

Notes

1. G. M. Trevelyan, "Clio Rediscovered," in Fritz Stern, ed., *The Varieties of History* (New York: Vintage Paperback ed., 1973), pp. 227-45.

2. Henry and Sidney Cowell, *Charles Ives and His Music* (New York: Oxford University Press, 1955), p. 105, and David Wooldridge, *From the Steeples and Mountains* (New York: Alfred A. Knopf, 1974), p. 216. Wooldridge erroneously identifies Langinger as the "former top engraver to Universal/Vienna."

3. One of Schmitz's most ardent admirers was Virgil Thomson, who recently reaffirmed his high opinions of Schmitz's piano playing. Moreover, Thomson feels that Schmitz was never properly recognized for his contributions to piano technique. (See Thomson interview, Oral History, American Music No. 42, Yale University.)

4. See the preface to Vivian Perlis, *Charles Ives Remembered: An Oral History* (New Haven: Yale University Press, 1974), for a description of the Ives Project.

5. The Schmitz Collection, discovered in 1969 after interviews in Montreal with Monique Schmitz Leduc, daughter of Germaine and E. Robert Schmitz, includes letters, photographs, files, and memorabilia. Of special interest are letters between Schmitz and many well-known composers. The Langinger Collection, discovered during interviews in 1975, consists primarily of transactions between composers and New Music Editions concerning publication. These papers were left with Langinger by Henry Cowell and include correspondence, proof sheets, bills, and several music manuscripts.

6. Gustave Reese, *Music in the Renaissance* (New York: W. W. Norton, 1954), p. xiii.

7. Wilhelm Dilthey, *Collected Works* (Stuttgart: Teutner Verlag, 1914).

8. Hans Meyerhoff, ed., *The Philosophy of History in Our Time* (Garden City: Doubleday Anchor Books, 1959), p. 10.

9. Darius Milhaud, *Notes Without Music,* transl. Donald Evans (New York: Alfred A. Knopf, 1953) p. 50.

10. Schmitz also worked with Félia Litvinne, Emilio Gogorza, Julia Culp, and Lula Mysz-Gmeiner.

11. Langinger interview, Oral History, American Music No. 39, Yale University.

12. "On Armistice Day, I had been preparing some programs for a trip West and had not heard the news until I reached the street. I was completely engulfed, slapped on the back, embraced, kissed—literally carried off my feet. It was unbelievable and total hysteria." (Ornstein interview, Oral History, American Music No. 21, Yale University.)

13. Seeger interview, Oral History, American Music No. 1, Yale University.

14. E. Robert Schmitz, *The Capture of Inspiration* (New York: Wehye, 1935).

15. Leduc interview, Oral History, American Music No. 52, Yale University.

16. Langinger interview.

17. *The Metronome,* February 1929, p. 55.

18. In their biography of Ives, the Cowells place Langinger in Chicago at this time, when in fact he was already in New York.

19. Langinger interview.

20. On 24 August 1920 John Alden Carpenter wrote to Schmitz, "It is not to be expected that this particular type of American music should find at first very much favor in European countries, dealing as it does with an idiom which is unfamiliar and whose spirit is not fully understood." Carpenter then thanked Schmitz for his

work on behalf of the *Concertino,* with an explanation of his previous commitment to Percy Grainger for the first New York performances. (From a letter in the Schmitz Collection)

21. *New York World,* 24 December 1926.

22. From a letter of Thomas A. Edison to Schmitz, 9 July 1920. (Schmitz Collection)

23. Leduc interview.

24. From a letter of Prokofiev to Schmitz, 13 November 1925. (Schmitz Collection)

25. Historians Warren Susman, Robert A. M. Stern, and Josephine Herbst.

26. André Siegfried, *America Comes of Age* (New York: Harcourt, Brace & Co., 1927)

27. Pro-Musica Diary, p. 41. (Schmitz Collection)

28. From a letter of Ravel to Schmitz, 12 January 1927. (Schmitz Collection)

29. *Ibid.*

30. From correspondence between Bartók and Schmitz. (Schmitz Collection)

31. Winthrop Tryon, quoting Schmitz, in the *Christian Science Monitor,* Boston, 6 June 1925.

32. "The Folk Music of Hungary," *Pro-Musica Quarterly,* 1928.

33. Alistair Cooke, "Remembrance of Things Past," in *A Generation on Trial* (New York: Alfred A. Knopf, 1950), pp. 3-41.

34. *Ibid.,* p. 41.

35. George Orwell, "Inside the Whale," reprinted in *A Collection of Essays* (New York: Doubleday & Company, Inc., 1954), p. 236 of the Anchor Paperback edition.

36. From a letter of Schmitz to Ives, 26 November 1931. (Ives Collection, John Herrick Jackson Music Library, Yale University)

37. From a letter of Ives to Schmitz, undated. (Ives Collection, John Herrick Jackson Music Library, Yale University)

38. Pro-Musica Diary. (Schmitz Collection)

39. Leduc interview.

40. Milhaud, *Notes Without Music*, p. 196.

41. E. Robert Schmitz, *The Piano Works of Claude Debussy* (New York: Duell, Sloan and Pearce, 1950).

42. Duluth *News-Tribune*, 22 July 1934.

43. Monique Schmitz married one of her father's talented students, Jean Leduc. Both worked closely with Schmitz at the school and with the Debussy competition.

44. Langinger interview.

45. Langinger interview.

46. (New York: Simon and Schuster, 1937).

The Institute for Studies in American Music at Brooklyn College, established in 1971, is a division of the Department of Music in the college's School of the Performing Arts. The Institute contributes to the field of American-music studies by publishing a monograph series, bibliographies, and a newsletter. It encourages and supports research by sponsoring fellowships for distinguished scholars and is currently supervising the series *Recent Researches in American Music,* published by A-R Editions, Inc. I.S.A.M. activities also include concerts held at Brooklyn College for students, faculty, and the public. In addition to serving as an information center, the Institute participates in conferences and symposia dealing with all areas of American music, including art music, popular music, and the music of oral tradition. In 1974, I.S.A.M. co-sponsored (with Yale University) the Charles Ives Centennial Festival-Conference and, in 1977, The Phonograph and Our Musical Life, a conference exploring the humanistic impact on our musical culture of the phonograph and sound-recording in general.